woodware

ÅKE R. NILSSON

Translated by D. Cook-Radmore

woodware

DRAKE PUBLISHERS INC
NEW YORK

ISBN 0–87749–438–X

LCCCN 72–10742

Published in 1973 by
Drake Publishers Inc
381 Park Avenue South
New York, N.Y, 10016

Printed in Great Britain

Contents

NOTE ON MEASUREMENTS

The dimensions given in this book are not critical, and are only intended to give an approximate idea of the size of the objects shown. The following conversion table may be of help.

Millimetres	Inches	Millimetres	Inches
1	0·03	140	5·51
2	0·08	160	6·30
3	0·12	180	7·09
4	0·16	200	7·87
5	0·20	220	8·66
6	0·24	240	9·95
7	0·28	260	10·24
8	0·31	280	11·02
9	0·35	300	11·81
10	0·39	320	12·60
20	0·79	340	13·39
30	1·18	360	14·17
40	1·57	380	14·96
50	1·97	400	15·74
60	2·36	420	16·54
70	2·76	440	17·32
80	3·15	460	18·11
90	3·54	480	18·90
100	3·94	500	19·68
120	4·72		

Easy-to-remember key measurement:
1 inch = 25·4 mm, exactly.
10 mm (1 cm) = ·39 inch

The treen, or small articles made in wood, shown in this book are meant not to be copied slavishly, but to provide ideas and inspiration for the reader's own creative designs. A main purpose of the book is to encourage the use of timber from fruit trees and ornamental trees, and to offer advice on how to go about collecting the timber, drying it and so on. A full description of laminating and simple dowelling is given, as well as a simplified and not excessively time-consuming method of removing waste timber.

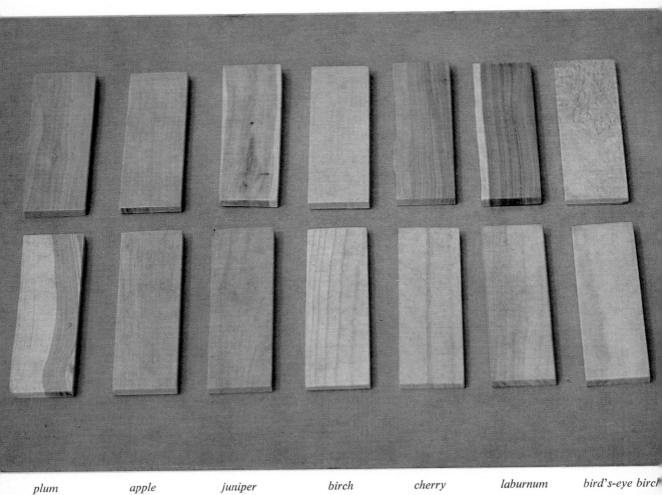

| plum | apple | juniper | birch | cherry | laburnum | bird's-eye birch |
| lilac | elm | pear | pine | copper beech | alder | lime |

Obtaining the timber

The wood of fruit and ornamental trees is usually burnt or thrown away when an orchard or garden is thinned out. Yet if the trunk of a laburnum, or a cherry-tree or pear-tree is cut in half down the middle, the discovery of how infinitely beautiful the wood of these trees can be will be enough to stop anyone interested in making treen from willingly discarding the timber. The wood is outstandingly suitable for making household woodware, and in most cases better than the imported "noble" woods. Work in wood, both in schools and for the amateur working at home, would gain a great deal from an increased use of these timbers, and be given a fresh impetus. Even in towns, many schools are reasonably near to municipal parks and gardens, and a teacher who makes friends with the Parks Department may find that, when trees are thinned or lopped, a generous supply is his for the taking—and the children will surely enjoy collecting it. If a fair amount of work is done before using these types of timber, word will soon get around and the workshop will never go short of material—in fact, everyone seems to be surprised and delighted to find that the waste timber can be put to good use.

Drying the timber

Newly felled timber contains about 30% moisture. When it has been stored out-of-doors, protected from the rain, so that the moisture content of the wood balances that of the surrounding air, it is termed "air-dry"; in this state, the moisture content is about 20% in winter and a little less during the summer months. If air-dry wood is then taken indoors and kept for some time in a centrally heated room, the moisture content will drop to about 5% and the wood is then said to be "room-dry". Drying timber in this way takes a long time; in the furniture and woodworking trades the process needs to be completed very much more quickly, so artificial drying methods are used. For the amateur who does not have access to a steam-drying plant, the only possible solution is to first air-dry the timber, and then finish off the drying in a warm room.

This matter of drying is indeed the greatest problem, although some of the difficulties can be circumvented by working on the wood direct while it is in the "green" state. Most of the bowls and ladles shown in the book were made from green timber.

It is virtually impossible to air-dry round timber without it splitting. The wood of fruit-trees and ornamental trees is often spirally grown to a marked degree, with the direction of the fibres failing to run along the lengthwise axis of the trunk. When a spirally grown log is dried, a long split can appear, running around the whole trunk; timber which has split in this way is practically useless for woodworking purposes. So it is wise to saw timber through the centre while it is still "green"; it will then be able to alter shape (shrink) during drying without appreciable cracks occurring. To avoid drying cracks at the ends of the log, where the timber dries fastest, the end-grain can be painted with a thick coating of glue, and a sheet of paper laid over this while it is still wet. The timber should be stored outdoors under cover for the whole of the summer, shielded from the sun and with free air circulation; it can then be brought indoors and kept at room temperature for a few months before it is used.

Laminating pine

Once upon a time it was possible to pick and choose timber for one's woodwork, selecting straight-grained, fine-looking heartwood. The modern woodworker, who must rely on the timber-yard for his materials, usually has to make do with the outer "sapwood". It is not generally possible to saw up a tree-trunk to give more than two to four planks of heartwood. Heavy building timber is always taken from the heartwood, and this is the reason why the woodworker finds this kind of timber so scarce.

The photograph below shows a pine log that has been sawn through. The two centre planks are heartwood, with the annual rings running vertically. The cut passing directly through the centre of the trunk is called the radial cut, and the others tangential cuts. In planks produced by the latter—the side or outer planks—the annual rings run increasingly horizontal the farther the cut is away from the centre of the log. Heartwood is twice as strong, and works (i.e. shrinks or swells) only half as much as sapwood.

Sawn pine log

A joined sheet of heartwood has a much smoother and more attractive texture and a more brilliant surface than a joined sheet of sapwood. Heartwood thus has many advantages; but as we have seen it is in short supply, and to supplement the limited amounts available we can employ a technique known as laminating.

Laminating involves piling planed planks of, say, 20 mm thickness one on top of another with glue sandwiched between them, and then pressing them hard together between cramps to set. If the heartwood sides of the planks are laid facing the same way, the texture will be smooth. Sheets of the desired dimensions are then sawn from the block, and joined together to obtain the required width (see illustration).

We now have a board with vertical annual rings which, from the point of view of strength, smoothness and fineness of texture, is comparable to heartwood—you can see, in the photograph above, the rough, loose texture of the sapwood plank and the tight, smooth texture of the laminated board.

Laminating pine. The block on the left is built up from 20 mm planks glued together. A board sawn from the block lies in the centre, and a pine plank of sapwood on the right.

Dowelling

Nowadays there are glues which set very quickly and give a very strong bond, and the excellent properties of these glues should be utilized to simplify the process of jointing. In the past a set of shelves, for example, always had first to be rabbeted or dovetailed—a difficult and time-consuming task. The modern woodworker wants quick results. An example of simplified construction is the use of dowel pins in jointing. The spice rack seen in Fig. 64 was made by this method. First, the shelves are glued to the end-cheeks. When the glue has set, two 6-mm holes are drilled through the cheeks and into each shelf, from the outside, spaced at about 20 mm from the front and rear edges of the end-cheeks (if the shelves are deep, several holes can be drilled). Glue is brushed into the holes, and a 6-mm dowelling peg is then dipped in thin glue and driven into the hole; the hole should be at least twice as deep as the shelf is thick. This is the simplest method of dowelling. Dowels help to strengthen the joint, and can be made of a different type of wood from the article itself; the commonest material is beechwood. They can easily be made by the woodworker himself, starting from a square rod which is planed and filed until round and finally driven through a 6-mm hole drilled in a piece of hard wood.

Another and rather more complicated way of dowelling our shelves would be to drill into the end-cheeks from the inside, to a depth equal to three-quarters of their thickness. Matching holes are drilled into the ends of the shelves, and dowels of the correct size glued into place; the shelves are then glued to the end-cheeks in the normal way, giving a strong and invisible joint. The difficulty with this method is to line up the holes in the end-cheeks and shelf-ends accurately with each other. This can be done by driving pairs of nails into the ends of the shelves where the holes are to be drilled, cutting off the ends of the nails with pincers to leave about 2 mm projecting, and then offering up the shelves to the end-cheeks and pressing the whole unit together. The unit is then taken apart again, and when the nails are pulled out they will leave guide marks for drilling the shelves and end-cheeks.

From bole to bowl

Once timber has been dried it is very much harder than in its sappy state. This is particularly true of the wood from fruit and ornamental trees, which becomes rock-hard. Sappy timber can be used for some treen—e.g. for making scoops and bowls that are not turned on a lathe. Preferably the wood should be worked on while completely green—hollowing out a bowl from raw timber is child's-play compared to the same task on dried wood.

It is most important that work on sappy timber should continue uninterrupted. First the bowl is hollowed out, and then the outside is shaped so that the walls have the desired thickness—the thinner the better. The wood will shrink, or "work", considerably during drying, but if it is no thicker than 2–3 mm shrinking will not as a rule lead to cracks. If the wood is thin, it can "work" without resistance. It will not do to hollow out the bowl one day and leave work on the outside until the next—the stresses in the wood as it dries will be so great that cracks will inevitably occur. If work has to be interrupted, the part-finished bowl can be kept in a sealed plastic bag. The pinewood bowl seen in Fig. 55 was stored in this way, as an experiment, for more than two months between working on the inside and outside surfaces, and did not crack. Wherever one of the articles shown here was made in this way, the caption mentions that it was "worked from sappy, raw or green timber".

Two blocks of pine-
wood. That on the left
has the heartwood side
uppermost, while the
right-hand block has
the sapwood side on top.

Dishes in pinewood.
The blocks for the dishes
were cut one after the
other from the same
plank. They are identical
in shape. The left-hand
dish was hollowed-out
from the heartwood
side, the right-hand one
from the sapwood side.
It is thus possible to
obtain a totally different
appearance, depending
on which side of the
block is hollowed out.
You are working with
the wood when
hollowing-out the
heartwood side, and
against it when working
from the sapwood side.

There are various ways of tackling work on dishes. One method is to saw the block to the overall shape of the dish, then hollow it out, and finally work on the outside. The difficulty here is that the dish can easily be broken when it is clamped to the bench and beginning to get thin.

Another way is to screw a holding block to the upper side of the dish, and grip this in a vice. First work on the outside, then unscrew the block and glue another block to the bottom of the dish. To make later removal of this second block easy, a sheet of paper (glued on both sides) can be sandwiched between it and the dish.

18

Gluing

The art of gluing materials together was known to the Egyptians 4000 years ago, and furniture grave-goods from the Pyramids are found to have been assembled using animal glue (i.e. made from bone or hide). This glue is not waterproof, but as the Egyptian climate is so dry traces of it have survived to the present day. Since the Second World War, animal glue has given way to synthetic adhesives, such as PVA, phenol formaldehyde resins and urea formaldehyde resins.

Vinyl adhesive is a thermoplastic glue that softens when heated. It is very simple to use; you merely brush it on, then immediately bring the two surfaces together and keep them pressed together for 10–20 minutes. The result is a completely invisible joint which is, moreover, stronger than the surrounding wood. Like animal glue, vinyl adhesive is not waterproof, so it cannot be used for outdoor jobs.

Phenol resin glue, on the other hand, is waterproof. It has to be mixed with a hardener before use. This means that the period over which it can be applied is limited, and it must be used within 1–2 hours (depending on the air temperature at the time—the warmer the day, the quicker it hardens).

An important point to note is that phenolic resin glue cannot be used at an air temperature lower than $+5°$ C. Even before the hardener has been mixed in, it has a limited shelf life of from 3 to 6 months (depending on the storage temperature).

Phenolic resin glue gives a completely watertight joint that is impervious to boiling, but is slightly coloured. Its applications include, in particular, boat-building, garden furniture and, in general, any kind of joint that will be exposed to wind and weather.

Cellulose glue is a fast-drying, colourless adhesive that gives a hard, brittle joint. It is best suited to model-making, and is excellent for joining glass and chinaware; it is not recommended for gluing furniture.

Contact adhesive is a rubber glue, excellent for joining glass and metals as well as for fixing plastic laminates of various types to wood (e.g. kitchen chopping-boards and worktops). The glass of the hand mirrors seen in Fig. 9 was fixed with contact adhesive. *N.B.*: contact adhesive *must not* be used for gluing wood to wood, as the joint is then far too apparent and not particularly strong.

Finishing the surface

It is essential that the article should be carefully smoothed-down and wet-sanded before a start is made on staining, glazing and varnishing or any oiling of the surface. Stains, varnish or oils will never conceal a poorly prepared surface—quite the opposite, they show up any carelessness in smoothing.

Wet-sanding involves brushing the smoothed-down article with a small amount of hot water, just enough to make it damp. The fibres of the wood will swell with the damp, and after it has dried for a few hours the raised fibres can be rubbed down with a clean sheet of Grade 00 glasspaper. This stops the wood from roughening and the fibres from swelling during subsequent finishing. All glasspapering should be done along the grain.

Most of the articles illustrated were given a protective surface finish. No dye was used (except on five items that were glazed), and the wood's own colour and texture have been used to advantage.

Oiling. Polishing with oil is an old and well-known method of treating wood. It is very simple to do, gives a matt satin finish and makes the wood somewhat more resistant to dirt and moisture. An oiled wood surface dries out after a while, and can be revived with a fresh application of oil; any dirt spots can first be rubbed off with Grade 00 glasspaper or washed away with turpentine.

The oil is applied liberally with a linen rag so as to saturate the wood, and the wet surface is rubbed down with Grade 00 glasspaper and then wiped clean. A further coating of oil is applied, and after an hour the surface is wiped clean and dry. After drying for 24 hours, the surface is burnished with a brush to give a matt satin finish.

Linseed oil, diluted 1:1 with turpentine, provides perhaps the most lasting finish, but after some time it gives the wood a yellowish tinge.

Medicinal **liquid paraffin** can also be used. This has no colour, taste or smell, and is hence suitable for use on objects that come into contact with food.

Important: rags or cotton waste that have been soaked in linseed oil present a serious fire risk, since they can easily ignite spontaneously. Either burn them, or keep them in a closed metal box.

Glazing. If, for some reason, you want a colour different from that of the wood, yet still to keep the texture, you can either glaze or stain it.

Glazing—painting the wood with oil colour diluted with turpentine to about the consistency of thick cream—is done direct on the wood or on an undercoat of opaque colour (see below). If it is applied direct to the wood, the texture will show through. At least two coats are needed for a satisfactory result, rubbing down lightly with Grade 00 glasspaper as soon as the first coat has dried; when the surface has been brushed clean, the second coat can be applied using a rather thicker colour. It must be worked into the wood as evenly as possible with a round-section paint brush. Care must be taken that the colour really does act as a glaze, i.e. that the texture of the wood shows through, and coats must be applied thinly. To finish off, the colour should be smoothed out with a flat-section stipple brush.

Another method is to paint on the oil colour and then wipe it from the wood with a linen rag, repeating the process a number of times. This is perhaps the simplest way, but as wood sometimes absorbs the colour unevenly the result may be patchy.

If, for some reason, your wood is discoloured ("blue" wood or the like) the glaze can be applied on an opaque undercoat. This can be in a light tone, while the glaze coat is darker. While the glaze coat is still wet, a brush, the fingers or some other means may be used to create a pattern effect following the shape of the object.

Staining. There are two types of stain—dye stain and chemical stain. In both cases the wood is painted with a liquid and allowed to dry, after which the surface is given a protective finish of linseed oil or clear varnish.

Dye staining is done with an aniline dye powder dissolved in water, ammonia or methylated spirit.

Water dyes are dissolved in warm water, and used on new wood.

Ammonia dye is dissolved in concentrated ammonia; the amount required is stirred in until it forms a thin gruel, and water is then added in accordance with the instructions for use. Ammonia stain is used on woods containing tannic acid (such as oak) and on woods that are so oily that a water stain will not "take".

Spirit dyes are dissolved in and diluted with methylated spirits. They can be mixed into varnish or polish for improving the appearance of old furniture that has been stained previously. Worn edges on old articles of wood can be touched up with spirit stain.

Full instructions for making up these stains will be found on the packets.

In **chemical staining,** also known as acid staining, chemicals act on the wood to produce a variety of colours and shades.

Chemical staining is particularly suitable for pine, and there are several mixtures giving different results; here we shall limit ourselves to one formula that gives the yellow tone of old pinewood.

The wood is first painted with pyrogallol solution (10 g pyrogallol in 1 litre of water) and then, when it has dried for several hours, with potassium chromate (1 g dissolved in 2 litres water).

When the wood is dry, a dilute solution of ammonia (1 part concentrated ammonia to 7 parts water) is applied. When the article has dried for 24 hours in a light room, it can be varnished or oiled.

The chemicals needed can be bought from a chemist's shop. In general, the stains should be applied liberally. Dye stains can be applied with either brush or sponge, chemical stains only with a brush (which should not have any steel parts, as they will cause discoloration; nor must a steel container be used for stain).

Varnishing. Varnishes are bought ready for use. There are clear and coloured varnishes, but when varnish is mentioned in this book only the clear variety is intended: this usually takes the form of cellulose varnish or polyurethane varnish. Polyurethane varnish has been used on the articles seen in this book; it is unaffected by water or alcohol spirit, is scratch-resistant, and does not discolour with exposure to light. Some polyurethane varnishes need a "hardener" additive, and this is enclosed in the package. Varnish to which hardener has been added must be used at once.

There are two ways of using clear varnish. One is to fill the pores of the wood, applying at least two coats and rubbing down lightly with Grade 00 glasspaper between coats; the other is to polish the surface with thin varnish, painted on liberally and then quickly wiped off with shavings or a linen rag. Several of the turned articles in this book were coated with varnish which was then wiped away with shavings while the article rotated gently in the lathe. The varnish was diluted 5:1.

Varnish is sold as glossy, semi-matt or matt, and the latter two types are recommended. It should be diluted slightly before being painted on with a good-quality brush (preferably badger-hair), applied in a band the full width of the well-loaded brush and then at once brushed out evenly. As it dries very quickly, any going-back to touch it up can spoil the surface. The can will usually give a complete description and detailed instructions for use.

81 Articles in wood, with photos and text

All dimensions shown are in millimetres
(See also note on page 8)

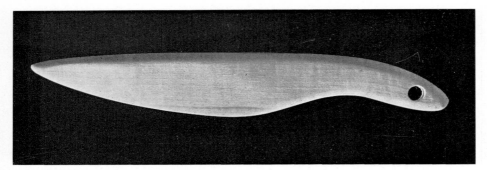

1 Paper knife in lilac.
Length 160, width 25.
Polyurethane varnish.
A paper knife should be designed so that a book or a letter is slit open smoothly and swiftly. The blade needs to be thin and sharp-tipped, and a hard wood such as lilac or bird's-eye birch should be chosen. A paper knife with softly rounded edges and a surface polished until it has the feel of soft silk can be a pleasant companion when reading a new book.

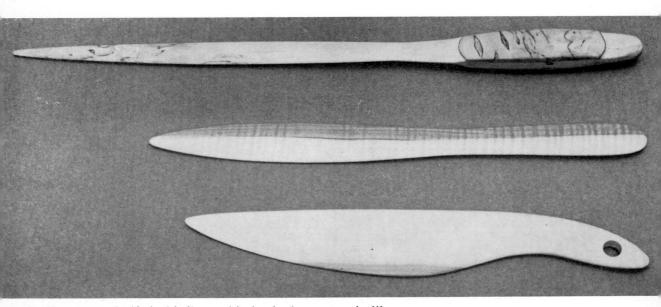

2 Top paper knife in bird's-eye birch, the lower two in lilac.
Length of top knife 245, blade width 10.
Polyurethane varnish.
Maple is a good substitute if bird's-eye birch cannot be obtained.

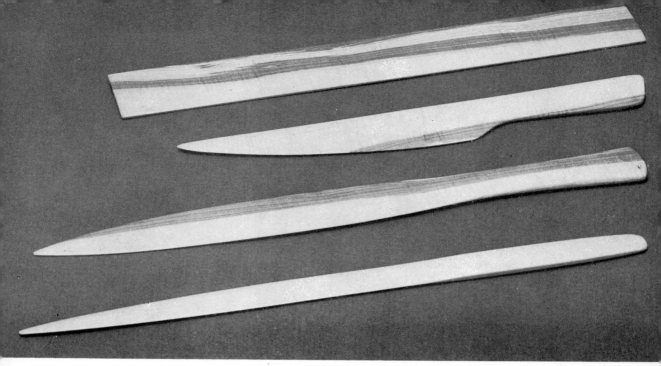

3 Rule and paper knives in lilac.
Rule: length 300, width 35.
Polyurethane varnish.

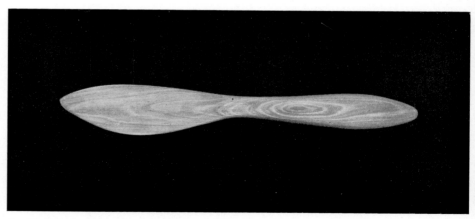

4 Butter knife in juniper (see p. 49).
Length 160, width 24.
Polished with liquid paraffin.

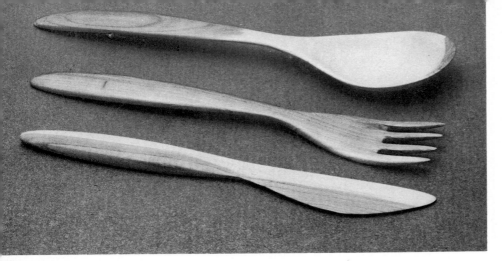

5 Knife, fork and spoon in lilac.
Spoon: length 200, width 47.
Fork: length 200, width 33.
Knife: length 200, width 25.
Polished with liquid paraffin.
This set can be used with the alderwood plates seen in Fig. 57.

6   Ham servers.
Upper server in applewood.
Length 280, width 52.
Surface untreated.
Lower server in laburnum.
Length 240, width 50.
Polished with liquid paraffin.

7   Salad servers in pearwood
Length 300, width 55.
Polished with liquid paraffin.
The servers were sawn to shape in one piece which was then split in two. Both
parts were hollowed out, and the left-hand one sawn to make the fork.

8   Coat peg in applewood.
Length 260, width 90.
Surface untreated.
An example of how natural shape
can be utilized.
The rear is planed flat for easier
fixing to the wall.

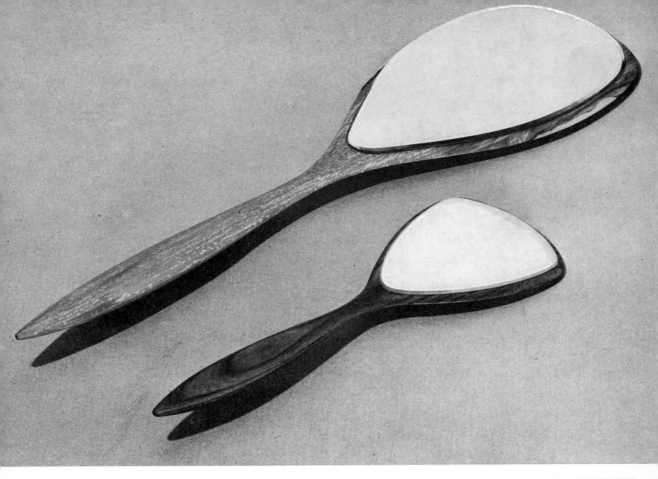

9   Hand mirrors.
Larger mirror in applewood.
Length 435, width 125.
Smaller mirror in laburnum.
Length 255, width 90.
Polished with linseed oil.
The mirror glass has been
bevelled, and stuck to the wood
with contact adhesive.

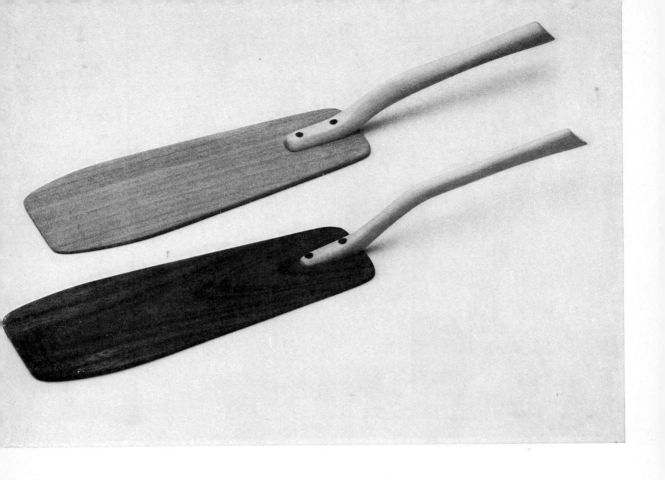

10 Pie servers in laburnum and pearwood, with lilac handles.
Length 260, width 57.
Polished with liquid paraffin.
Handles glued and dowelled (see dowelling, p. 15)

11 Bread-board in birch with applewood handle.
Length 550, width 135.
Polished with liquid paraffin.
Made from untrimmed timber, with edges debarked and smoothed. The handle
is a natural-grown branch of applewood, pinned through and wedged.

12 Bread-board in pine with birchwood handle.
Length 395, width 240.
Polished with liquid paraffin.
Laminated pine has been used for this bread- or cheese-board (see laminating, p. 13). The handle is glued, bored through and dowelled (see dowelling, p. 15).

13 Tray in laminated pine.
Length 610, width 265, thickness 5.
At least two coats of polyurethane varnish.
The handles were cut from either end of the same blank and glued to the top of the tray, so that the grain pattern continues into the handles. Strips 5 mm thick have been glued to the side edges.

14   Tray in laminated pine.
Length 415, width 235.
Polyurethane varnish.
Made in the same way as the tray in Fig. 13.

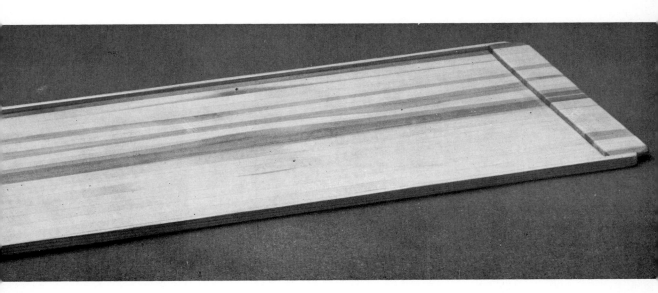

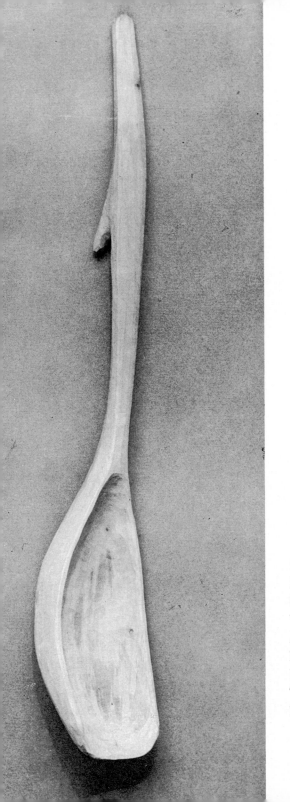

15 Spoon in limewood.
Length 700, width 120, thickness 100.
Surface untreated.
Worked from sappy timber (see p. 16).
A large spoon. In Scandinavia it would be used for ladling water in the sauna.
It could of course be scaled down.
There is a hook on the back of the handle for hanging the spoon.

16   Spoon in applewood.
Length 550, width 105, thickness 40.
Polished with liquid paraffin.
Worked from sappy timber.
Made from a natural-grown blank, retaining its curved shape; can also be used as a serving-spoon for sweetmeats.

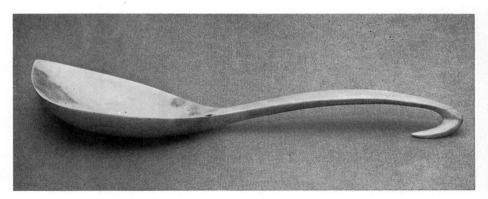

17   Spoon in limewood.
Length 370, width 100, thickness 50.
Surface untreated.
Worked from sappy timber.
Spoon for right-handed person. The left corner is rounded, the right corner right-angled, making it easier to scrape out a pan.

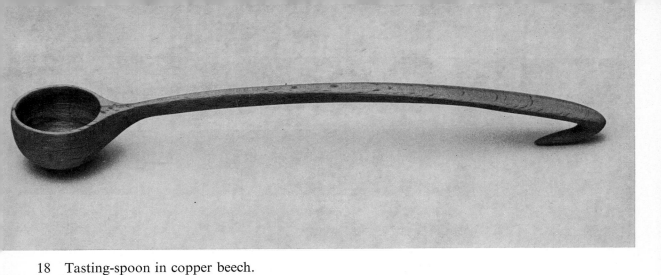

18   Tasting-spoon in copper beech.
Length 350, width 45, thickness 50.
Polished with liquid paraffin.
The point of using copper beech is that this has neither taste nor smell.

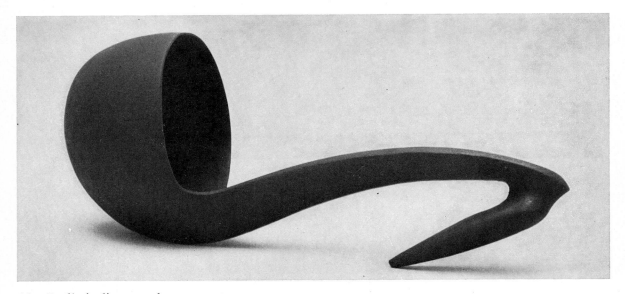

19   Ladle in limewood.
Length 210, width 75, thickness 100.
Glazed.
Worked from raw timber (see p. 16)

20 Spoons in laburnum, of various sizes and shapes.
Polished with liquid paraffin.
Worked from sappy timber.

Laburnum is rare among woods. It has a truly golden colour, an interesting grain and a lustre that makes it specially suitable for small treen such as spoons bowls and hand-mirrors.

The deep-bowled spoon is carved from raw timber, using an unusually thick branch of laburnum that has made it possible to achieve a new and different shape—it has the appearance of a spoon, while serving the function of a bowl. A new shape calls for a new name—the "spowl". Since the branch was curved in two directions, the spoon was shaped to follow the lines of the original wood. The heartwood comes at the centre-point of the spowl.

21   Spowl in laburnum.
Length 430, width 75.
Worked from sappy timber.
Polished with linseed oil.

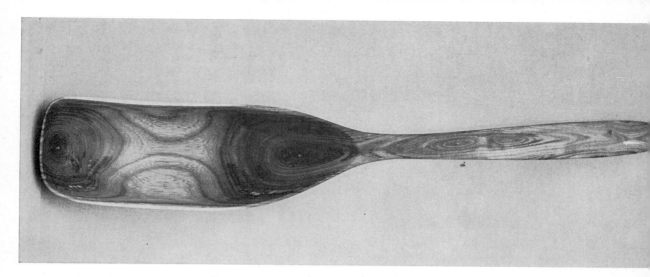

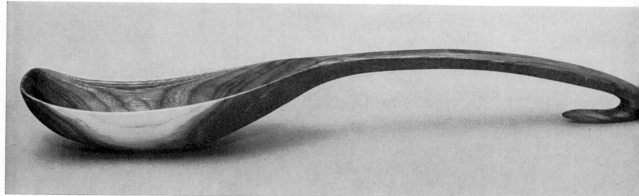

22 Spowl in laburnum.
Length 430, width 70.
Polished with linseed oil.

23 Ladles in laburnum.
Larger ladle: length 160, width 60.
Smaller ladle: length 110, width 45.
Polished with liquid paraffin.
Worked from sappy timber.

24 Ladle in laburnum.
Length 240, width 140, thickness 70.
Polished with liquid paraffin.
Worked from sappy timber.

25 Salt spoons in laburnum.
Larger spoon: length 100, width 19.
Smaller spoon: length 65, width 15.
Polished with liquid paraffin.

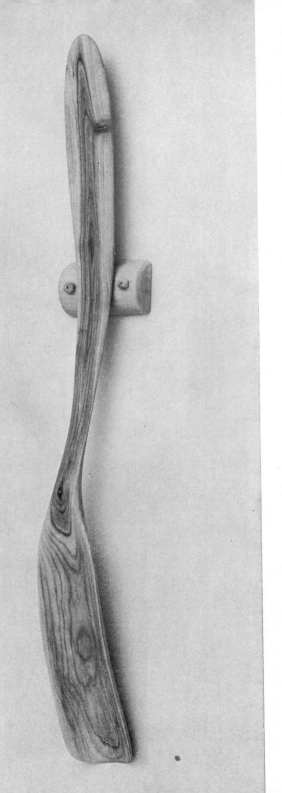

26 Shoehorn in cherrywood.
Length 560, width 45.
Polyurethane varnish.
Made from a split branch of cherry. A twig at
the back has been shaped into a hook for hanging the shoehorn on its holder, seen in the detail
photograph.

27   Shakers in applewood.
Salt and pepper shaker, height 90.
Sugar shaker, height 200.
Polished with liquid paraffin.
The shakers have been shaped from branches that have been drilled out. Thin discs of wood, drilled with sifter holes, have been glued to the tops; the light-coloured wood is for salt and sugar, the dark wood for pepper. The shakers are filled from the bottom, through filler holes fitted with wooden plugs.

28   Table-napkin-ring in plumwood.
Length 115, width 42, thickness 17.
Polyurethane varnish.

29   Small turned pot in applewood.
Height 40, diameter 65.
Polyurethane varnish (see p. 22).
The pot is first turned, smoothed and polished
with varnish; the smoothing and polishing can
be done while it rotates slowly in the lathe. It
is then separated from the stock with a parting
tool. Next, the inside surface of the lid is shaped,
with a flange to fit the mouth of the pot. The
outer surface of the lid is turned down as far as
possible, smoothed and polished in the same way
as the pot, and finally parted from the stock and
finished off by hand.

30　Mortar and pestle in pearwood.

Height 95, diameter 90.

Polished with liquid paraffin.

Both mortar and pestle are turned on the lathe. The sides and base of the mortar need to be massive, so that it will stand firm during grinding with the pestle. The latter is shaped to match the inside of the mortar, which is deeply curved at the bottom.

31 Turned salt cellar and spoon in laburnum.
Height 40, diameter 50.
Polished with liquid paraffin.

32 Turned cigarette box in laburnum.
Height 90, diameter 75.
Polished with polyurethane varnish.
If an object is to be turned on the lathe and a
suitably thick piece of timber is not available it
is possible—as with this cigarette box—to saw
a 2-inch (50 mm) plank in half down the centre.
The two halves are then planed and glued together, with the sawn edges facing the same
way, to give a glued block the two halves of
which are identical. The cigarette box was
turned by the same method as the pot in Fig. 29.

33 Spice jars in pearwood.

Height 80, diameter 63.

Polished with liquid paraffin.

These spice jars and their lids were, in each case, turned from the same block. A recess has been turned into the top of the lid to display the contents of the jar, the spices being stuck into the recess with contact adhesive; shown in the photograph are black and white peppercorns, cloves and ginger. A disc of cork is glued inside the lid to fit snugly into the mouth of the jar and provide an effective seal. The jars were made to fit the spice rack shown in Fig. 64.

34   Left: box in pinewood.
Height 70, width 75.
Polished with liquid paraffin.
The lid is formed from four pieces of end-grain glued together, while the sides
have glued joints. The lip to locate the lid is made from thin strips of the same
wood as the box, glued to the inside.

Right: box in bird's-eye birch.
Height 60, width 75.
Polished with silver (Zapon) lacquer.
Construction as for the pinewood box.
Bird's-eye birch is an exceptionally beautiful wood, but is difficult to work.
Maple, another decorative wood, may be used if bird's-eye birch is unob-
tainable.

35 Box in juniper wood.
Length 105, width 80, height 30.
Surface untreated.
The box has glued joints, with a divider across the centre.

Juniper is an unusual wood, with a very characteristic scent. The tree is tough, pliant and slow-growing; because of its slow growth it is fine-textured but difficult to obtain in large-sized pieces. At one time children used it to make bows. It is used for making butter dishes, because butter does not go rancid in these as quickly as in dishes made from other woods. Chests of drawers were lined with juniperwood to protect the clothes against moths, which dislike its smell.

Nowadays we use juniper for making small everyday objects, for the sake of its beautiful appearance and fresh scent.

One species of juniper, *J. virginiana*, flourishes in its native America where it has been known to attain a height of 100 feet. Western Red Cedar (*Thuja plicata*) might be used as a substitute if juniper cannot be obtained.

36 Candlesticks in pearwood.
Largest: height 335, thickness 70.
Smallest: height 180, thickness 45.
Polished with liquid paraffin.
All these candlesticks were taken from the
same piece of timber, to give a uniform
appearance when they are placed together.
Brass cups for the candles are in drilled
recesses.

37 Candlestick in plumwood.
Height 200, width 170.
Surface untreated.
Made from the natural form of a forked
branch, debarked with a knife and roughly
rounded on all edges. The brass cups for
the candles are in drilled recesses.

38   Kitchen tool rack in pearwood.
Height 370, width 340, thickness 8.
Polyurethane varnish.
An old and popular way of hanging up kitchen knives and spatulas. Two strips
of wood 10 mm thick and 25 mm wide are separated at each end by a block
5 mm thick, to form a slot for the knife blades. The strips are held in place by
screws through the back of the wall panel.

39   Tool cupboard in pine.
Height 740, width 520, depth 250.
Chemical-stained (see p. 22).
The tool cupboard is made from laminated pine (see p. 13) with birchwood fittings. Perspex windows are fitted in front of the gouges and chisels. The doors are hung on 8-mm wooden hinge-pins, capped with a knob at the top, and nylon washers are recessed into the baseboard so that the doors can swing easily without rubbing. The tools contained in the cupboard are sufficient for producing most of the articles shown in this book.

The cupboard contains:
- 6 chisels of various sizes
- 6 wood bits from 5 mm to 25 mm
- 6 gouges from 2 mm to 25 mm
- 16 drills from 1 mm to 10 mm
- 1 wooden jack plane
- 1 metal smoothing plane
- 1 pr pincers
- 1 screwdriver
- 1 scraper tool
- 1 folding rule
- 1 pencil
- 1 knife
- 1 scriber
- 1 bradawl
- 1 spokeshave
- 1 woodcarver's mallet
- 1 rasp
- 1 half-round file
- 1 flat file
- 1 handsaw
- 1 coping saw
- 1 set square
- 1 straight scraper
- 1 palette scraper
- 1 carpenter's brace
- 1 cork block
- 1 nail punch (nail set)
- 1 screw countersink
- 1 screwdriver bit for brace
- 1 hammer
- 1 marking gauge

40   Chopping-board in pinewood.

Length 290, width 220, thickness 38.

Polished with liquid paraffin.

The chopping-board is sturdily proportioned, so that steak can be beaten on it. Cubes of wood, measuring 38 × 38 × 38 mm, are glued together so that the end grain forms the top and bottom surfaces of the board; a waterproof glue was used (see p. 19). The chequerboard pattern was obtained by gluing the blocks together in a random arrangement, paying no attention to which way the heartwood and sapwood sides were facing (cf. Fig. 41).

41 Butter board in pinewood.
Length 145, width 95, thickness 11.
Butter knife in juniper (see Fig. 4).
Polished with liquid paraffin.
Assembled and glued in same way as chopping-board in Fig. 40.

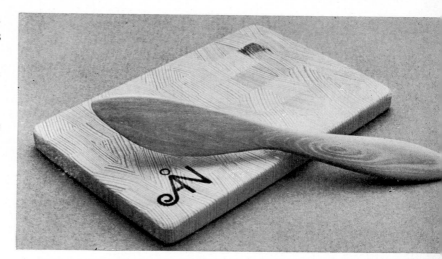

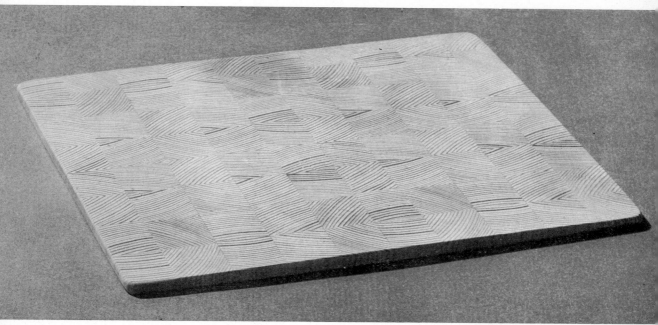

42 Casserole tablemat in pinewood.
Length 250, width 180, thickness 9.
Polished with linseed oil.
Glued together in the same way as the chopping-board in Fig. 40. The striped pattern has been achieved by facing the heartwood sides of the wood blocks towards each other.

43 Table lamp in pine with shade of self-adhesive plastic sheeting.
Height 260, diameter 95.
Polished with polyurethane varnish.
The lamp base was turned, smoothed and polished while still on the lathe. The shade consists of a plastic-covered wire frame. Two lengths of self-adhesive plastic sheeting (available from handicrafts shops) are shaped to the frame, and thin pressed flowers are sandwiched between the adhesive surfaces; a cloth is then laid over the whole, and the two sheets pressed together with a warm iron. The material is stuck to the frame with cellulose adhesive.

44 Wall lamp with swinging arm.

Arm in birchwood, length 820.

Polished with polyurethane varnish.

The lamp comprises a wall-plate with a slot cut in it to carry the arm. A 6-mm hole for a hinge-pin is drilled through the upper jaw of the bracket, through the arm and some way into the lower jaw. A 15 × 15-mm groove has been sawn along the arm, into which a sliding part is fitted. The inner end has a slot channelled out for the electric flex. The arm has a 4-mm-thick strip glued over the groove. The shade is made of thin strips of pine, height 210, width of sides at top 96, width at bottom 175.

Surface of pine strips untreated, top board polyurethane varnish. A 1-mm groove was sawn in the top board 8 mm in from the edges, and the two outer pine strips on each side slotted into this. The middle strip was then glued on to the two outer strips, with a 5-mm overlap. A 7-mm hole was drilled through the top board for the electric flex.

45   Wall lamp with shade, in pine.

Wall-plate: length 175, width 55, thickness 12.

Arm: length 175, width 55, thickness 15.

Polyurethane varnish.

The arm is attached by screws through the back of the wall-plate, and a hole for the flex is drilled through the wall-plate and the arm, with grooves along the arm and down the rear of the wall-plate.

Shade in pine.

Height 175, width 130.

Surface untreated.

The shade consists of strips of pine $1\frac{1}{2}$ mm thick and 20 mm wide, glued to each side of 3×5-mm ribs.

46 Bed lamp in pine.
Length 230, height 120, depth 90.
Polyurethane varnish.
The top and sides are glued. Thin pine strips, sawn with sloping grooves to take the pinewood louvres, are glued to the front edges of the sides. The back is a sheet of 4 mm plywood, and ventilation holes are drilled in the top.

47 Lampshade in pine.
Height 350, diameter 120.
Surface untreated.
Strips of pine, $1\frac{1}{2}$ mm thick and 20 mm wide, are glued together round the outside of a 4-inch (100 mm) drainpipe or a similar former: the strips are tightly held in position with rubber preserving-jar sealing rings while the glue sets.

A 3-mm-wide chamfer is planed along the strips to provide a wide, overlapping surface for gluing.

A pinewood cross is glued to small blocks inside the top of the shade, and a 7-mm hole drilled through it for the electric flex.

48   Stool in pine.

Length 620, width 300, height 480.

Glazed with oil colour, 2 coats (see p. 21).

The seat is made from a single untrimmed 50 mm plank. The sloping sides of the plank have been retained, and carefully smoothed down with all edges well rounded. The heartwood faces upwards. The legs are 50 mm square, tapering to 25 mm, and are tenoned right through the seat and wedged from above.

49 Stool in pine.
Length 620, width 300, height 470.
Chemical stain and polyurethane varnish (see p. 22).
The seat is cut from the same untrimmed plank as in Fig. 48, but this time the heartwood faces downwards. The sloping sides have been kept; all edges are smoothed-down and well rounded. The legs are 62 × 50 mm in section, tapering to 25 mm at the bottom. They are tenoned into drilled sockets and wedged, but do not pass completely through the seat.

50   Round stool in pine, *right*.

Height 450, diameter 380, thickness of seat 58.

Glazed, two coats.

A pine plank, with a length rather more than twice the intended diameter of the stool and a width equal to just over the diameter, is scribed with two squares (whose sides are thus slightly more than the diameter of the stool). The diagonals of these squares are drawn, and the plank sawn up along the diagonals. Four of the resulting eight pieces are arranged and glued together to form a square with the grain of each piece running towards the centre. This block for the seat can then be sawn to a circular shape and turned in a lathe, and the final result will have a uniform and interesting grain pattern (see cover photograph in colour).

The lathe-turned legs are tenoned into drilled sockets, but do not pass right through the seat.

51   Square stool.

Length of side 300, thickness 58.

Glazed, two coats.

The four pieces remaining after making the round stool can be made into a seat with a different pattern; this time the stool is square, and the grain runs parallel to the edges. It can also be used as an occasional table.

An example of how things can be made when they are wanted, under primitive conditions and with tools as simple as a saw and a knife. This chess-set was made while on military service, with ink the only material available for staining the black pieces.

The pawns were carved with a knife from a 25 mm square length of timber, then sawn off and finished. The other pieces were made in the same way from timber 31 mm square.

52   Chess-set in alderwood.
Pawn: height 34, side of base 25.
King: height 78, side of base 31.
Finish: the black pieces were painted with ink, and the white eyes cut out.

53 Mobile of bark boats with birchwood sails.

Boats: length 50, beam 11, height 16.

Sails: height 55, width 21.   Surface untreated.

The boats and sails are trimmed with a knife, and the sails stuck down into the
hulls and glued. The boats hang on nylon thread, and the mobile can be sus-
pended in various ways.

54 Bowl in limewood.

Length 230, width 100, height 75.

Glazed, two coats (see photo on cover).

Worked from green timber.

This bowl was made from round timber. Lime is an excellent wood for those aiming at a more sculptural shape, and is easy to work with a knife and other tools. Since limewood is quite brittle and soft compared to the wood from other broad-leaved trees, the articles should be made rather thicker and more solid.

55 Bowl in pine.
Length 380, width 180, height 180.
Glazed.
The bowl was hollowed out from green timber, the whole diameter of the trunk being used so that the heart runs along the middle of the bowl. As a result, the annual rings form an identical pattern at each end.

This was worked from green timber at intervals, as an experiment; in the intervening periods it was kept in a plastic bag to prevent it from drying, as described on p. 16.

56 Bowl in applewood.
Length 195, width 80, height 70.
Polyurethane varnish.
Like the previous bowl this was worked from green round timber. As a complete
log was used, the heart runs through the middle of the bowl and the annual
rings can be clearly seen, giving the same pattern at both ends.

57 Plates in alderwood.
Deep plate: diameter 200, thickness 30.
Shallow plate: diameter 200, thickness 25.
Polished with liquid paraffin.
Turned, smoothed and polished in the lathe in one operation.
The knife, fork and spoon shown in Fig. 5 match these plates.

58   Cheese-board in elm.
Diameter 355, thickness 38.
Polished with liquid paraffin.
A large solid cheese-board providing plenty of room for bread and cheese or open sandwiches.

59   Bowl in birchwood.
Diameter 280, thickness 45.
Polyurethane varnish.
Turned from a solid birch plank, and smoothed and polished in the lathe.

60 Bowl in alderwood.
Diameter 290, height 65.
Polished with liquid paraffin.
The bowl was turned from a 75 mm plank.

61 Bowl in pine.

Diameter 220, height 180.

Polyurethane varnish.

Two-inch planks were glued together to give a billet the same width as the intended diameter of the bowl. As four slabs glued one on top of the other were needed to give the right height, the length of the plank had to be rather more than four times the diameter of the bowl. The timber had to be dried, and to reduce stresses in the plank and prevent the bowl from cracking at a later stage, the plank was split lengthwise through the centre and glued together again.

(As the heart sometimes did not run parallel to the sides of the planks, the lines of the glued joints were offset during lamination of the blank for this bowl.)

The bowl has a massive, solid shape, so the sides and base are quite thick—about 15 mm and 35–40 mm respectively. The inside of the bowl is deeply rounded at the bottom.

62   Bread-dish in alderwood.
Diameter 250, height 125.
Polished with liquid paraffin.
Two 75 mm alder planks were glued together to give the necessary thickness.
The dish was turned, smoothed and polished in the lathe in a single operation.
The decorated edge was produced by drilling 7-mm holes and then cutting out
with a knife.

63 Cake-stand in birchwood.
Height 430.
Bottom tray; diameter 280, thickness 30.
Top tray: diameter 175, thickness 30.
Polyurethane varnish.
An example of how a drawing or picture can provide inspiration. The author's son Anders saw an unfinished sketch of a bread-dish on the drawing board, became interested and took it to his school woodwork class, where he produced his own design for a stand that can be used to carry different kinds of cake at a tea-party.

64 Spice-rack in pearwood.

Length 500, max. depth 120, height 410.

Polyurethane varnish, two coats.

The end-cheeks are to a personal design. At the bottom a gutter-shaped bar has been provided for hanging ladles and spoons. The shelves have a curved front edge, and are about 20 mm deeper in the centre than at the sides. A sort of guardrail is fitted above the lower shelf, joined to it by rods carved to the artist's own design. For details of assembly, see "Dowelling", p. 15.

Salt and sugar shakers (see Fig. 27).

Spice-jars (see Fig. 33).

Three spoons (see Fig. 20).

Two ladles (see Fig. 23).

Tasting spoon with long handle (see Fig. 18).

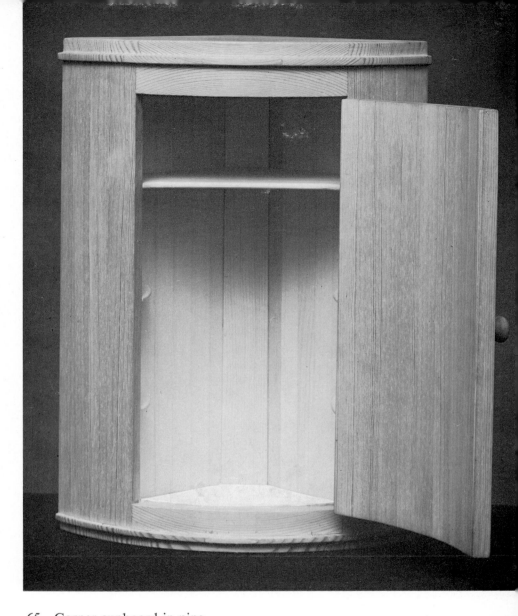

65   Corner cupboard in pine.
Height 430, width 300, depth 200.
Chemical-stained and polished with polyurethane varnish.
Like the tool cupboard in Fig. 66, this is made from laminated timber and
assembled with glue and dowels. Hinges and door-knob of lilac.
Fitted with a large shelf at the top and two side shelves, 5 mm thick.

66 Wall cupboard in pine.
Height 390, width 300, depth 105.
Chemical-stained and polished with polyurethane varnish.
Made from laminated pine (see p. 13), with hinges and door-handle in lilac.
The hinges are glued on to the cupboard, and reinforced with dowel-pins (see
p. 15). The design was inspired by the traditional "spirits cupboard": the shelf
at the top, for glasses, has a cut-out at the centre to accommodate the necks
of the bottles, and there are small shelves for glasses on either side.

Detail of hinge of cupboard in Fig. 65.
Length 100, width 18. thickness at hinge-pin 12.

Detail of hinge of cupboard in Fig. 66.
Length 68, width 16, thickness at hinge-pin 8.

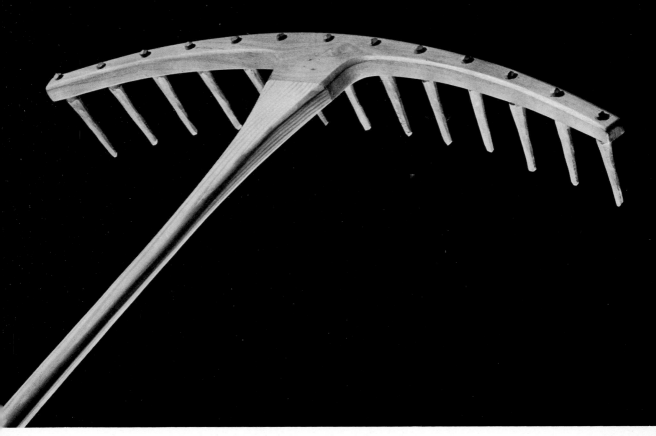

67   Rake in applewood and spruce.

Length 1830, width 520.

Polished with linseed oil.

The rake has a spruce handle, with head and teeth of applewood.

A rake must be curved in two directions if it is to work properly. When the head is laid on the ground it should rest on the two outermost teeth with the teeth at the centre some 20 mm clear of the ground. Conical holes are drilled for the teeth. To ensure that they will not work loose, the wood for the teeth is stored in the dry indoors and the material for the rest of the rake outdoors; the teeth later swell and are gripped firmly.

A wooden rake is hardly needed for trimming the modern suburban lawn once a week, but for country dwellers it is ideal. To feel the slim, well-shaped handle slide through one's hands and hear the characteristic sound of the stubble as it swishes between the rake teeth is the very epitome of high summer.

Special terms used

Dovetailing. Making a right-angled joint (e.g. at the corners of a drawer) by means of interlocking, wedge-shaped tongues and slots.

Hardener. An additive mixed with phenolic resin adhesive before use, to make the adhesive harden or "set". Also used with polyurethane varnish.

Joined board. Several planks are butted edge-to-edge (the edges having been planed smooth and square) and glued to form a single sheet.

Rabbeting. The edge of one piece of wood is fitted into a groove cut in another piece.

Sappy or green wood. Timber that is recently felled and full of sap, rendering it easy to work.

Tenoning. A hole, or mortice, is drilled in one piece of wood and a round pin, or tenon, at the end of another piece, is pressed into it, glued and wedged.

Texture. The appearance of the finished surface of the wood, i.e. its "grain pattern".

Through-tenon. The tenon reaches right through the morticed part, and is visible from the other side.

Index